Come Blow Bubbles With Me

DEDICATION

I dedicate this book to my amazing daughter
Aamori, she brings so much joy and
happiness to my life.
She is six years old and her playful ways
inspired me to write this book. My child is
such a fan of bubbles
we got every bubble gadget you can think of.
This book is field with imagination and
adventure. A great
book for beginner readers, a lot of sight
words too. The character was created to
look like my daughter
and its wonderful. I hope you and your family
enjoy this book and expect more to come!

COME BLOW BUBBLES WITH ME

Written by: Genesis Wilder

Illustrated by: Ananta Mohanta

I blow bubbles in the house

I blow bubbles in the yard

I blow bubbles wherever i can

I blow bubbles in the bed

I blow bubbles in the street

I blow bubbles with my dad

I even blow bubbles on my feet

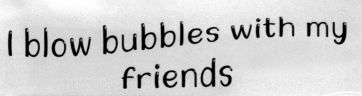

I blow bubbles with my friends

I blow bubbles with my dog

I blow bubbles to the sun

I blow bubbles in the closet

I blow bubbles just for fun